Block chain: The Comprehensive and Essential Guide to Understanding and mastering the Hidden Economy (Block chain Technology, Fintech, Investing in Ethereum, Smart Contracts, Financial Technology, Internet Technology)

By:

Rick Loftus

Published by 42 Enterprises Publishing,
All Rights Reserved,
Copyright 2016, Cincinnati, Ohio

Table of Contents

Introduction 3

Chapter 1: The Blockchain Currency 4

Chapter 2: The Reinvention of Financial Services 9

Chapter 3: Smart Contracts 15

Chapter 4: Ethereum 18

Chapter 5: Limitations of Blockchain Technology 23

Conclusion 29

Introduction

Over the last few years, a new, self-regulated economy has been slowly coming up on the internet thanks to an alternative currency called the Bitcoin. Bitcoin is basically a digital currency that is used on the internet in a decentralized system that uses a public leger called the Blockchain.

The Blockchain could be the answer to a problem the internet has had for a long time, the lack of an economic layer that could be used to facilitate payments, increase spending, allow people to acquire and transfer digital assets more easily, and allowing companies and individuals to issue and execute smart contracts. In fact, Blockchain and the Bitcoin could be so influential in the near future that they completely change the way thatwe do business completely, and change our lives in much the same way that the internet did in the last few decades.

Bitcoin has no central authority like most of the other currencies on the planet, which has helped it gain trust among internet users since it was created. One of the reasons why the currency has become so popular is because users do not need to trust each other. Thanks to self-policing, users are not able to con the system, and any attempts to do so are automatically rejected. Since its inception, there have been a number of other currencies that have been created to try and challenge Bitcoin and the Blockchain. However, none have managed to achieve the same reach, and none have become as popular as Bitcoin.

This book looks to cover some of the most important aspects of the Blockchain and bitcoin, and introduce you to the increasingly popular financial revolution.

Chapter 1:
The Blockchain Currency

Most internet users are familiar with Bitcoin, however, the term Bitcoin is confusing because it refers to three different aspects of the digital currency. Bitcoin refers to the currency itself, Blockchain technology, and the protocols that are used to govern the transfer of assets within the Blockchain.

The Blockchain is the ledger that contains all the records of different transactions that take place using the different cryptocurrencies like Bitcoin. It is basically a database that is shared by all the nodes in a network, and is updated by data miners across the globe. However, the best thing about the Blockchain is that it is not owned by anyone, which means that it cannot be manipulated in the same way that banks manipulate currencies. The fact that it is not owned by anyone means that everyone has access to the records, and any and all updates that are made can be viewed by everyone. It also means that anyone can verify that their transactions are genuine, and block any transactions that seem suspicious.

Blockchain protocols are the software programs that facilitate the transfer of assets over the Blockchain leger.These programs help to transfer Bitcoins, or the currencies themselves. There are hundreds of other cryptocurrencies out there, but they are all fundamentally imitations of Bitcoin, which happens to be the largest and oldest of all the cryptocurrencies out there.

It is important to note that these three aspects of Bitcoin remain the same regardless of the cryptocurrency they are using. Each coin represents both the currency and the protocols that govern it, and may run on either its own

Blockchain or the Bitcoin Blockchain. For example, Lite coin, a modification of Bitcoin, runs on the Lite CoinBlock chain which has basically the same structure as the Bitcoin Blockchain. However, there are other currencies that run on the Bitcoin Blockchain, such as Counterparty, which despite the fact that it is an independent currency, is traded on the Bitcoin Block chain.

The fact that these currencies all work in basically the same way allows for the different currencies to use the same Blockchain. They all have basically the same components: software developers that develop the protocols used by the blockchain, data miners, merchant processing services, online wallet companies, exchanges, and the users of the currencies. Depending on how you look at it, the most important elements when it comes to trading in the different currencies are addresses, private keys and online wallets.

Addresses are the places where bitcoins can be sent, while private keys are the encryptions that are used to send coins to others. Online wallets are the different types of software that individuals run from their computers to manage their cryptocurrencies. As there is no centralized account system, users need to register with other companies to be able to manipulate their accounts. If you have the private keys to an address, you can use that key to access the bitcoins on that address using any internet-enabled device, including smartphones and tablets. Wallet software also maintains a copy of the blockchain, allowing users to gain access to all the transactions that have taken place in that currency, and verify any of the transactions that take place.

There are many aspects of blockchain technology that many blockchain users are not used to, such as backing up their money. The fact that the currencies are decentralized means that there is little or no customer service whatsoever, especially in terms of backing up private keys and recovering passwords. For this reason, there are quite a few bitcoin users that have lost their funds due to the fact that they have either misplaced their private keys or their passwords.

There are many people who believe that this makes bitcoin technology flawed, and therefore unsuitable for use by the masses. However, there are companies that are trying to address this issue by trying to create a series of standardized applications or services that can be used to backup information such as private keys so that users can confirm exactly what is happening with their accounts.

The fact that many people believe that bitcoin technology is still in its infancy means that there are very few companies that are actually willing to trade in the currency. This is because it is quite difficult for companies to set up two different payment systems, one for Bitcoin and another for traditional forms of payment. One of the only ways to fix this is to integrate the bitcoin payment system into current payment systems, especially mobile payment systems that will allow bitcoin users to make purchases using their mobile phones or tablets. There are already a few companies working on these systems, but there is still a lot of work that needs to be done if making purchases using bitcoin is to become a viable option across the board.

There is also the problem of the exchange rate between bitcoin and normal currency. For instance, at its peak, one bitcoin was trading at $1,242, $2 more than an ounce of gold at the time. The prices may have dropped, but the problem persists, and it is compounded by the fact that there are very few real world vendors that are willing to trade in bitcoin, as well as users who are using bitcoin for the purchase of goods and services.

The volatility of the bitcoin also plays a major role in the slow widespread adoption of the cryptocurrency. There are companies that are trying to address this issue, such as Bit reserve, which locks bitcoin deposits at fixed exchange rates. There are also companies that are allowing the bitcoin to be pegged to the price of gold or silver, rather than currencies as has been the norm.

The fact that there is very little government regulation of the bitcoin also plays a major role in the adoption of the currency. As it stands, there are a number of countries that have completely banned the trade in bitcoin, including Bangladesh, Ecuador, Bolivia, Vietnam and Kyrgyzstan. China banned financial institutions from trading in bitcoin, however, ordinary citizens can still trade and transact with the online currency.

A number of countries have discouraged the use of the currency, including Germany, France and Korea, while countries like the US, Canada, Poland and Switzerland are still discussing different Bitcoin-related issues. The problem is that they are trying to match up the bitcoin to their own currencies, which is virtually impossible as the way cryptocurrencies are set up mans that they cannot fit into the usual financial structure, which means that new legislation has to be drawn up to address the concerns of legislators.

However, there are countries that have classified bitcoin as a currency, such as the UK. There are other countries that have tried to classify bitcoin as a currency, such as Australia, but they have not been able to due to different laws that restrict them from doing so.

As it stands, the Internal Revenue Service in the US views bitcoin as property, much like stocks, meaning that unlike in the UK, bitcoin in the US is subject to taxes such as capital gains tax. However, there are certain government agencies, including the Financial Crimes Enforcement Network, the CFPB, CFTC, SEC, DOJ and banking regulators that view the bitcoin as a legitimate currency.

Chapter 2:
The Reinvention of Financial Services

From its inception, bitcoin was seen as something much more than a currency and a way to facilitate payments. For this reason, the possibilities for programmable money and contracts were included in the protocols from the start. The protocols were designed to support a wide variety of possible transactions that could be carried out with the bitcoins, for instance, Escrow transactions, bonded contracts and third-party arbitration. This is because should the currency actually catch on, there are a myriad of different avenues that people will want to be able to explore. However, these avenues needed to be developed from the onset, so that once the time comes they can be explored without having to redesign the whole system.

Blockchain 2.0 is the next step in the development of the blockchain industry. The fact that it is still in development means that there are many different ways that it can be understood and categorized. For this reason, there are new definitions and classifications being created every day including Bitcoin 2.0, Bitcoin 2.0 protocols, Smart contracts, Smart property, Dapps (decentralized apps) DAOs (Decentralized Autonomous Organizations) and DACs (Decentralized Autonomous Corporations).

Blockchain 1.0's main focus was the decentralization of money and payments, allowing users more control of their finances. However, Blockchain 2.0 focuses more on the decentralization of markets, and looks to address the transfer of different assets using the blockchain.

Think of blockchain technology the same way you would the internet. When the internet was first created, the technology and infrastructure to make it what it has become were all available, and it was up to different companies to take advantage of the technology put in place to make it work for them. That is how companies like Amazon, Netflix and eBay have managed to become so sophisticated over time, they are just finding new ways to take advantage of the technology that has been there from the beginning.

Therefore, Blockchain 1.0 can be seen as the TCP/IP layer of the web, and Blockchain 2.0 as the protocols that take advantage of this layer, such as HTTPS, SMTP and FTP. Blockchain 2.0 protocols utilize the standard bitcoin blockchains, though they can also run on their own separate blockchains. However, it should be noted that due to the fact that Blockchain 2.0 protocols are still in development, certain metaphors for the way they run could become obsolete in the future.

The idea behind Blockchain 2.0 is that the decentralized leger of the blockchain could be utilized to register, confirm and transfer a wide range of property and contracts. The vision is to have all financial transactions reinvented on the blockchain, including crowdfunding, trade in stocks and bonds, private equity, mutual funds, pensions and all their derivatives such as futures and options.

Public records can also be moved to the blockchain. Things such as property and land titles, business licenses, marriage certificates, and death certificates can all be registered and traded on the blockchain. Identities can be verified using securely encoded driver licenses, ID cards, passports, and voter registrations. The blockchain can also store personal records such as loans, contracts, bets, signatures, wills and trusts. Confirmation can be done through proof of insurance or ownership and notarized documents, while physical asset keys can be digitized and stored on the blockchain. This will allow users to control the access to everything from their homes and cars to hotel rooms and garages. Blockchains could also help people protect their intangible assets, such as patents, trademarks, copyrights and domain names. For instance, if a blockchain user were to encode the blockchain with their ideas rather than trademarking or patenting the idea, then they would have proof that the idea was theirs, complete with a timestamp if they ever need it.

Blockchain 2.0 is already being used to reinvent banking thanks to its versatility. For instance, Ripple Labs, a venture capital backed company, is already using blockchain technology to allow financial institutions to carry out their business more effectively. The payment network that the company has introduced to these institutions allows them to transfer their funds and carry out their foreign exchange transactions without having to involve a third party as is the norm. The company is also developing a smart contracts platform and language that banks and other financial institutions will be able to use to create contracts for their clients.

Other businesses are also beginning to connect bitcoin to different financial and payment market solutions. For instance, PayPal shares various attributes with bitcoin, and is actually in the process of adopting bitcoin as well. At its inception, PayPal was viewed in much the same way bitcoin is viewed today, as an alternative to traditional payment market solutions. However, it has slowly become a more formal business, and the fact that it has become more focused on corporate business means that it has now largely lost this image.

Some businesses are actually introducing bitcoin to the regulated financial services market. For example, Kraken, a bitcoin exchange, has teamed up with banks to help provide people with regulated bitcoin services. This is because they realized the need for users to be able to use bitcoins on traditional financial products and services more easily.

Another way in which Blockchain technology is revolutionizing financial services is in crowdfunding, and the way it is carried out. It is slowly becoming clear that peer-to-peer lending sites such as Kickstarter can replace the need for entrepreneurs to seek out venture capitalists. However, Kickstarter is rather centralized, and tends to act as a third party when it comes to crowdfunding. However, if people were to utilize blockchain technology to carry out their crowdfunding, they can cut out "middlemen" like Kickstarter. Using blockchains to carry out crowdfunding also allows people with startups to create their own digital currencies, and to carry out the sale of shares to early backer, where each investor receives a token that represents a particular number of shares in the startup.

There are currently a couple of cryptocurrency crowdfunding platforms out there, including Swarm, a startup that managed to raise $1 million during its own crowdfunding exercise that ended in the summer of 2014. Swarm created its own currency, the Swarm coin that investors can use to claim dividends on the company's portfolio. Lighthouse is another company that runs a crowdfunding platform using cryptocurrencies, except in this case it allows its users to run their crowdfunding using a standard bitcoin wallet.

Crowdfunding is one of the most high-profile topics during bitcoin industry conferences. This is mainly because there is still no legal framework in place to ensure that someone who buys shares in a startup using cryptocurrency will actually be awarded their shares. There is also a debate about the legality of crowdfunding with cryptocurrencies, especially in regards to current securities laws.

Certain companies have tried to offer a solution to this by selling items that cannot be considered shares to their clients such as access to unreleased software. However, there are some problems with this strategy, because at the end of the day it seems a lot like the companies are just selling shares anyway. This results in some investors getting nothing other than the software that they have been given. This trend cannot continue for long without bringing up complications, and for this reason a better method is needed, especially if people who would like to start crowdfunding using the blockchain technology want to ensure that they stay on the right side of the law.

The registration of assets via blockchains does not face the same legal issues. This is despite the fact that blockchains can be used to for any type of asset registry, including every area of finance, economics and money. Using blockchains in this way opens up a whole world of possibilities in business, especially when it comes to financial transactions. This is because any property encoded in a blockchain becomes smart property, which can be traded using smart contracts.

Property including houses, cars, and even computers can be made smart property. For instance, Swarm coin has a number of physical artworks that can be bought, and ownership transferred via the bitcoin blockchain. These artworks are controlled by whatever entity owns the private keys, which in this case is Swarm coin. Transfer of ownership of the assets is as easy as exchanging the private key with someone for a fee.

This method of transfer of ownership is especially useful to financial institutions like lending agencies and banks. This is because by using the blockchain, the transfer of assets can be automated. For instance, if you were to take out a car loan, depending on the smart contract, the vehicle title could be transferred to you automatically once you have completed the payments, saving you and the institution time and money.

This feature could also be useful to other industries. For instance, if you have a cell phone that you must pay for every month, by using a blockchain, the cell phone company could cut off access to its services automatically until you have made a full payment. You could also use this feature for security reasons. For instance, you could lock your phone and only have it unlock once the right digital identity has been entered. You could also set up the blockchain so that access to your home or office is only possible if the right digital code or software token is used.

Blockchain technology gives users the ability to completely change how authentication is carried out, which allows for more secure access to sensitive information and property. However, as it is a totally new concept, smart property will take a long time for people to get used to. There are also very many changes that may need to be made, especially to current laws and structures. For instance, as the ownership and transfer of smart property is dictated by code, it is self-enforced. This means that should a transfer be made, or a transaction be carried out, it can only happen according to the way the code has spelled it out. This means that there is very little room for deception, but it also means that there are a whole new set of implications to property law that need to be addressed.

Chapter 3:
Smart Contracts

The basic idea behind blockchain-based smart contracts can be gleaned from the discussion on smart property in the previous chapter. When discussing them in the blockchain context, smart contracts are blockchain transactions that are more than just buying and selling currency transactions, and many have more complicated instructions programmed into them.

Traditionally, a contract is an agreement between two or more parties, usually stipulating that something shall or shall not be done in exchange for goods and services. With standard contracts, each party must trust that the other will uphold their end of the agreement. However, with smart contracts, though the agreement between the two parties may be similar in that each agrees to do or not to do something in exchange for compensation, the need to trust the other party is removed from the equation.

This is because smart contracts are dictated by code, meaning that they are executed according to the code, regardless of any party's discretion. There are three different aspects of smart contracts that make them unique. These are Autonomy, Self-sufficiency and Decentralization.

Autonomy means that once a contract is launched and operational, no more contact is needed between the program and its creator. The Self-sufficient nature of these contracts stems from the fact that they can gain their own resources by providing services or issuing equity to raise funds. They can also redirect those funds to the places they are needed, such as storage. The Decentralized nature of these contracts means that they do not exist on one server alone, but are distributed across all the nodes in a network, and they can execute themselves.

The easiest way to illustrate this point is to think of a vending machine. Unlike a human, the machine can only operate according to the way it was programmed, and the same instructions will be followed by the same results every time, unless there is a serious software error. The same can be said about smart contracts. Once written, the contract has no choice but to execute the instructions within it, and it will execute those instructions to the letter the same way every time. This is a startling new development for society, and will require a lot of getting used to before it can become a widespread idea.

This is because there are many things that need to be considered when dealing with smart contracts, especially when it comes to the legal implications of these contracts, and ways in which they can be effectively regulated. A clear distinction needs to be made between the rigid smart contracts and the more flexible human contracts that are currently legally binding. However, this is not the only consideration that needs to be made, as smart contracts also change the way we do business on a social level. Decisions need to be made concerning which areas smart contracts can be applied to because of the way that current laws are worded. There are very few, if any provisions for the way that smart contracts are executed, and there is even less room for protest when it comes to these contracts. For that reason, it is important that the parties agreeing to a smart contract ensure that there is some sort of legal framework written into the code to ensure that no disputes between the parties arise. There could be multiple legal frameworks in a contract, in much the same way there are multiple different currencies across the globe.

Despite the fact that smart contracts do not necessarily make the impossible possible, they do allow for people to engage each other in a way that requires minimal trust. This means that people can take their judgement out of the equation, allowing for the complete automation of the contract. For instance, you can draw up a smart contract that states that an individual would finally be able to access their trust fund on their 21st birthday. The instructions can sit in the database for months or even years before they are triggered, usually by a specific event or time. However, before the contract is executed, a check is usually done to ensure that it has not already been carried out.

Another way you can use Smart contracts is when you need to make automatic payments. For instance, if you would like to place bets on your favorite sports team, a smart contract would be the perfect way to ensure that your bets are placed on time regardless of where you are. A smart contract or program can be written that allows for the automatic transfer of funds should something happen, or should a particular value is reached for a specified product or service.

Smart contracts can also be used for crowdfunding applications and websites like Kickstarter. For instance, you can set up a smart contract that will only deduct money from investors' wallets once the amount of money that has been pledged to you equals your fundraising goal. Additionally, you can further program the contract so that you will not be able to clear any transactions until all the funds are received. Your budget, spending and burn rate can be tracked by the block chain by tracking the outflow transactions from the account.

Chapter 4: Ethereum

The effects of blockchain technology may not be evident for a couple of years to come, but it is already beginning to change the way people think by allowing innovators to combine multiple concepts and operations from different fields. These fields include everything from computing and communications to cryptography and artificial intelligence. The creator(s) of bitcoin initially had three steps lined up for the development of bitcoin, of which only two have been implemented so far with bitcoin 1.0. These steps are the blockchain itself, and the protocols that go along with the blockchain.

These two steps may have been fine in the beginning when bitcoin was used to trade currency only, however, with the implications of the power of blockchain technology starting to come to light, the third step needs to be implemented for the system to function properly. This third step is a more robust scripting system, which will lead to Turing Completeness, or the ability to run any coin, protocol or blockchain. The creator(s) of bitcoin saw this step as crucial to achieving the ultimate goal, having programmable money and all the features needed for it to be a fully enabled currency. At the moment there a couple of projects that are working towards this goal, however, the one that stands out from the crowd the most is Ethereum.

Ethereum is a programing language and platform that was specifically designed to help build and publish distributed applications. More importantly, Ethereum is a cryptocurrency platform that is basically a Turing-complete virtual machine, which means that it can run any coin, script or cryptocurrency project. Most of the other projects that are trying to achieve this goal run as blockchains, or protocols running over block chains, or as metaprotocols running over protocols. However, Ethereum is the only one that runs as the actual underlying infrastructure that can run every block chain or protocol that it comes across.

Each node in the Ethereum network uses the Ethereum Virtual Machine to ensure that the execution of programs is as seamless as possible. Ethereum acts as the main Blockchain-agnostic and protocol-agnostic for application development, and it allows programmers to write smart contracts that can call a variety of other blockchains, protocols and cryptocurrencies. The platform has its own environment, and includes file serving, messaging, and reputation vouching. The first part of Ethereum is the Swarm (the Ethereum-Swarm, not Swarm, the crowdfunding website), which acts as the decentralized file serving method. The second part of Ethereum is Whisper (Ethereum-Whisper, not the Whisper app or any other similarly named project) which is the protocol that is used to transfer information between nodes on the network. The Reputation system is the last part of Ethereum, and is used to verify a user's reputation, and reduce the risks posed by people when they connect to unknown networks.

After its launch in 2014, the Ethereum network grew quickly, and has become one of Bitcoin's biggest rivals. However, despite its success, there have been a few concerns raised by users and information security experts alike. For instance, The DAO, the Autonomous governance platform that Ethereum uses for its transactions, had a string of code in it that allowed any user to transfer an unlimited amount of funds from the DAO. In the summer of 2016, one user used this loophole to disrupt the system by transferring about one third of the available funds from the public Ethereum DAO to a private one that only they could access. This disrupted systems for about one month, as the money could not be transferred from the private node until the programming of the DAO was changed. This reduced the trust that people had in the system, and the value of Ether, the Ethereum cryptocurrency, fell by about $6, meaning that many investors lost money on their Ether. However, once the problem was fixed the community began to thrive again and things are looking good for the network.

Due to the flexibility of the Ethereum network, there are many different ways in which it can be used. Though it is primarily used for its cryptocurrency, much like Bitcoin, it is also used by people around the world to conduct business thanks to the extensive use of smart contracts entrenched in the blockchain. Some of the uses for the Ethereum network include:

- For investment funding

- As a socioeconomic platform

- As an options exchange

- As a for artists and musicians to release their work, the most prominent example of which is Imogen Heap, who used the Ethereum network to release her 2015 single "Tiny Human"

- To control the Internet of Things such as smart locks

Ether is pegged to either the Gold Standard or fiat-backed currencies. To help deal with the fluctuation issues that the currency sometimes experiences, it is now possible for you to import government backed currencies like the Euro into the network. The smart contracts that are embedded in the blockchain mean that regardless of the currency, it will still follow the standards that have been set by the Ethereum Foundation.There are also plans in the works to create a digital bank using the Ethereum network, something that would greatly benefit users of the Ether currency and other cryptocurrency users alike.

As you can see, there is a progression in the way blockchain applications are developing. They all begin with currency transactions, and slowly move into other financial transactions and smart property, and finally to networks like Ethereum which have a complex structure of autonomous smart contracts that help to run and regulate the network.

However, as the technology is moving much quicker than the legislation that can govern or control it is moving, there are many concerns regarding the legality of these systems as time progresses. For instance, Ethereum is already forecast to have technical and legal issues going forward, not only because it is still a relatively new network, but also due to the security issues mentioned earlier.

The fact that Ethereum is so much more complicated than bitcoin means that there is a lot more that can go wrong, as was proven in June 2016. In fact, an article in the New York Times even went as far as saying that the current system was so complex that even people who know it well have difficulty describing what it is and what it is capable of. One of the reasons it is so complex is because of the number of smart contracts that the network currently employs.

As much as these contracts allow for easier, faster transactions, writing a solid contract seems easy in theory but is notoriously difficult in practice. In fact, even one of

Ethereum's largest supporters, Microsoft, has noted this difficulty. However, they are in the process of looking into ways to verify contracts to ensure that none of them have any loopholes like the one that was exploited in June.

However, despite this, Microsoft has already began integrating Ethereum into its systems. For instance, Microsoft has already granted the users of the cloud-based business service Microsoft Azure, access to third party tools that give these users the chance to not only experience blockchain applications, like stock trading and cross-border payment apps, but also to build with them.

Chapter 5:
Limitations of Blockchain Technology

The fact that the blockchain industry is still in its infancy means that there are quite a few limitations that need to be addressed before it can become truly mainstream. Some of these limitations are external, while others are internal. Some of these limitations are related to technical issues with the fundamental technology, the public perception of cryptocurrencies, especially with the events of summer 2016 and Ethereum, and government regulations (or lack of them).

Some of the biggest challenges that blockchain technology faces are technical challenges. The challenges are very clear for all the developers to see, however, they all have different solutions to the problems, and therefore lengthy discussions have to take place before a potential solution is found and implemented. Additionally, the programmers responsible for the blockchains do not all share the same level of enthusiasm for their product, especially when it comes to solving the current problems that will take the blockchain to the next level.

There are those that believe that once all the issues are fixed, the bitcoin blockchain will become the industry standard, and everyone will be trading with bitcoins at one point or another. This is mainly because it is the oldest of the cryptocurrencies, and the network is more extensive than any other in the industry. However, there are those who do not believe that to be the case, and are branching out and forming their own cryptocurrencies, like Ethereum, in order to try and address some of the issues that Bitcoin is facing.

One of the biggest technical challenges though is trying to find a way to increase the number of transactions that can be done per second. At the moment, bitcoin is very far from even coming close to the volumes that some other financial institutions (like VISA) can handle. If bitcoin was to be adopted as a viable alternative to fiat currencies at this point, it would fail as the network still cannot handle much more than 10 or 20 transactions a second.

Another issue that needs to be addressed include:

1. Throughput

The Bitcoin network has a major issue with throughput, or the number of transactions it can handle per second. Despite the fact that the developers of bitcoin state that the limit can be raised at any time, especially once demand grows, there is still a lot of concern. This is mainly because many outsiders cannot see how the transaction rate can be completed without increasing the size of the blocks in the chain. However, modifying the size of the blocks will only lead to more complications, especially in terms of size and blockchain bloat.

2. Latency

At the moment, every bitcoin transaction takes about 10 minutes to clear because there are so many checks and balances that the transaction has to go through before it can be confirmed. However, there are some that argue that to ensure that security is maintained at all times, the transactions should actually take longer, especially for large transactions. This is mainly to reduce the likelihood of a double-spend attack, which is basically a situation where bitcoins are spent in two different transactions before the merchant can confirm that they have received the funds.

3. Size and Bandwidth

The blockchain is currently quite large and is over 80GB at the time of writing. To make it even worse, it grows every day thanks to the different transactions that are carried out and recorded. For many people, especially first time users, it means that downloading the current database would take about one day, a really long time to wait for a download to complete. However, if the throughput was increased to the same rate as VISA or even Twitter, the size of the databasewould grow so large that it may become impractical to download. As it is, the database is so large it will not fit on most mobile devices.

Right now the bitcoin community refers to the problem as bloat, however, that tends to infer that users would like a small blockchain, which is very far from the truth. With the current system, the blockchain should be as large as possible, especially if you would like to increase transparency when it comes to transactions. However, it also needs to be accessed in a more efficient way to allow for more people to access it. however, doing that will lead to centralization, something that goes against the fundamental bitcoin principles.

There are those that have tried to advocate for data compression. However, this is not a viable option as it brings up its own complications, such as accessibility issues and increased security risks. This problem has led some developers to begin exploring new compression algorithms that will allow for the blockchain to be compressed, without compromising accessibility or security.

4. Security

There are a number of potential security threats that are still to be addressed by the developers of bitcoin and blockchain technology. For instance, there is a possibility that one of the miners could take over the whole system and double spend coins into their own account. The problem arises because the lack of centralization means that the largest mining pools control the majority of transactions carried out on the blockchain.

There have also been concerns about other ways in which double spending is possible, for instance, if a user was to declare that they had not received any funds to ensure that they were resent the funds, doubling their income. There is also the risk that malicious code could be entered into the system to allow for double spending.

5. Wasted Resources

Mining uses a lot more energy than people expect, and all of it is wasted. For instance, one estimate put wastage due to mining at $15 million per day, while others state that the value is actually higher than that. However, it can be argues that this wastefulness is actually what makes miners more honest, as they have to compete in a system that does not really reward effort in an effort to make any kind of gains. On the other hand, it can be argued that the waste is really unnecessary, as there is no benefit to it other than mining.

6. Hard forks and multiple chains

Some of the issues encountered by bitcoin involve the infrastructure itself. One issue is the creation of different blockchains and that with so many different blockchains around, it would be easier to launch an attack on the system's smaller chains. Another problem is that once chains are split due to versioning or administrative reasons, there is no way to simply merge the chains, or transact across forked chains.

There are a number of challenges that arise when trying to apply bitcoin to business models as well. Most business models do not really apply to bitcoin due to the decentralized model of the system, meaning that there can be no people taking a cut as transactions are being carried out. However, there are a number of profitable products and services that can be offered in the blockchain economy.

For instance, tools created to educate people on the functions and benefits of bitcoin are very profitable, as are products that are geared towards improving the worldwide banking system such as Ripple. Additionally, products that deal with implementation services, customer education, and other value added facilitations are profitable. However, there are still quite a few businesses that will not be profitable for years to come, and these are the businesses which people will need to study in order to figure out how to make them profitable on the blockchain.

However, perhaps one of the biggest challenges that blockchain faces is the public perception. At the moment, there are still people out there who believe that bitcoin is one of the currencies that is preferred by people who use the dark net, specifically those who are involved in illegal activities such as drug dealing and money laundering.

What these people do not understand is that bitcoin and the blockchain are essentially neutral, just like any modern technology. Just like all other technology, it is very easy to use it for either good or evil, however, it depends on the user, not the creators of the product. No one has ever denied the possibility of the blockchain being used for less than ethical activities, however, compared to the benefits of using the blockchain the risks are negligible. The passage of time should improve the image of bitcoin and the blockchain, especially as more people adopt mobile money services like Google Wallet and Apple Pay.

However, public opinion will not change if the theft, scams and scandals that pop up every few months and are related to bitcoin do not change. There are numerous bitcoin scandals that have come up in the last few years, and they involve everything from stories of shady elements using bitcoin to hide their funds, to the outright theft of bitcoins. However, as security of the blockchain increases, such concerns will become a thing of the past, and users will be able to use the blockchain with the knowledge that their funds are safe.

Conclusion

Many of the people who know about bitcoins think that they are only useful as a currency exchange and for making purchases online. However, there is a lot more to bitcoins and blockchains that people have not realized, and this book should hopefully have opened your eyes to some of the possibilities that are available to those that choose to pursue them.

Despite the fact that the technology seems to be perfectly suited for those people who are involved in finance, you should have realized by now that it is applicable in so many other places and industries. For the moment, blockchain technology seems like an interruption to the status quo. However, that is how most new technologies are seen before they are finally accepted for what they are. Therefore, it is important for us to look to the future, and realize that this technology is here to stay, and is here to change our lives for the better.

www.ingramcontent.com/pod-product-compliance
Lightning Source LLC
Chambersburg PA
CBHW070302190526
45169CB00004B/1504